True Ghost

Stories

*Haunted Buildings, Creepy
Forests, Spooky Tales And
Eerie True Ghost Stories From
The Scariest Places On Earth*

Jason Keeler

Table of Contents

Want FREE books?

Would you love FREE books delivered straight to your inbox every week?

How about non-fiction books on all kinds of subjects?

We send out FREE e-books to our loyal subscribers every week to download and enjoy!

All you have to do is join! It's so easy!

Just visit the link at the end of this book to sign up and then wait for your FREE books to arrive!

Introduction

I want to thank you and congratulate you for purchasing the book, "True Ghost Stories: Haunted Buildings, Creepy Forests, Spooky Tales and Eerie True Ghost Stories from the Scariest Places on Earth".

Are you a self-confessed horror freak? Are there few things you love better than a good horror story to tell around a campfire or at parties? Let's face it, ghost stories make for great conversation topics. A little macabre, sure, but entertaining nevertheless.

It is often difficult to explain what lives in the beyond, why certain paranormal activities take place the way they do, cold spots, mysterious happenings and the likes. It does not matter if you think ghosts are real or just a figment of someone's imagination. Everyone believes in a good horror story if it is spooky enough.

Strange happenings have occurred across the globe that there is no possible explanation for, things that are outside the reach of scientific clauses and reasoning. Apparitions, noises and EVP readings are things that point to the unknown, telling us it exists, yet science cannot provide a reasonable explanation as to why it might be true.

Leaving the debate, if ghosts exist or not aside for another day, let us take a look at some of the best ghost stories from across the world. For anyone with a good eye for horror, I have compiled the perfect anthology of a few real life ghost stories that will make their skin crawl.

Make sure you check for monsters under your bed, say a silent prayer before you go to bed and be wary of what lays in the dark, for this book compiles the spookiest, most eerie true horror stories of all time!

Thanks again for purchasing this book, I hope you enjoy it!

Chapter 1:

Ghost Stories from Spooky Places

Have you been alone in a room, yet felt as if someone was watching you? Have you felt something amiss or creepy as soon as you set foot in a certain room? If you haven't been through it, I am pretty sure you have heard of such unexplainable stories or occurrences from people who have experienced such eerie phenomenon first-hand.

Others who have been fortunate enough to not experience the unthinkable have relied on Stephen King novels and Hollywood classics to feed their fantasies.

Today, I am going to share some of the most spine thrilling and eerie ghost stories from around the world, so brace up. And don't turn off the light!

Waverly Hills Sanatorium

Originally opened as a two-storey wooden building in 1910, the Waverly Hills building that you see now was built in 1926. Throughout the early-to-mid 20th century, it served as a hospital for tuberculosis, when the disease was at its peak and quite prevalent among people. At that time, tuberculosis required patients to be placed in quarantine, or isolation, for it was quite deadly.

Due to mistreatment and mysterious experimental procedures that took place there, it is said that over 63,000 patients perished in the hospital. Due to its alarmingly high death toll, the Waverly Hills sanatorium is considered one of the most haunted buildings in America.

The most interesting and spooky part of the sanatorium is the Body Chute, also known as the Death Tunnel. If the name wasn't indication enough, wait till you hear what it was used for. To prevent the existing patients from seeing the dead bodies of those who couldn't make it, a rail-car was used to transport these bodies from the top to the bottom of the hill. The tunnel is rumoured to be haunted by the dead.

As the Sanatorium allows people to investigate the quarters, some crazy evidence has showed up over the years, even making it on popular TV shows such as Ghost Hunters, Ghost Adventures, Most Haunted and the likes. Evidence shows thermal imaging footage of someone walking down the hallways, which turned out to be the ghost of a boy named Tim, often spotted in the premises before.

Aside from thermal imaging footage, there are also reports of apparitions, spine chilling screams, cold spots, fleeting shadows and disembodied voices.

A popular happening related to the sanatorium is that of Mary Hillenburg's death. In 1928, she was found in Room 502, hanging from the doorway, supposedly having committed suicide after finding out that she was pregnant with the child of a married doctor. However, later reports suggest that the suicide was in fact, staged by the doctor, as Mary had already succumbed to her death during the abortion he performed on her.

The sanatorium is open for visitors, but proceed with caution if you ever plan to go there, as visitors have often claimed to have felt cold shivers and heard voices down the tunnel.

Bhangarh Palace

Located about 220 kms from the nation's capital Delhi, Bhangarh is widely regarded as one of India's most haunted places. In ancient times, Bhangarh served as not just the king's residence but also as an entire town, which now remains in mere ruins. The place has so many stories of horrific events and spooky incidents happening in and around it that the fort in Bhangarh has a sign next to its main gate that reads;

"Entering the borders of Bhangarh before sunrise and after sunset is strictly prohibited. Legal action could be taken against anybody who does not follow these instructions"

Does that pique your interest yet? If your government declares a legal notice prohibiting anyone from entering the place's premises post-sunset, that's as clear indication as any that maybe the place really is spooky after all.

The fort of Bhangarh has various folklores associated with it, however, two stand out as the most popularly recognized and believed. The first one deals with a saint called Balu Nath, who used to reside in Bhangarh before the fort or king's residence was constructed. As per local folklore and myth, Balu Nath was a monk who had decided to dedicate his life to God, and was apparently against the notion of building a city near his residence, as he believed that the commotion would cause him unrest and disturbance in his prayers.

On much persuasion by the then king, Bhagwant Das,

Balu Nath agreed to let the city be built, but on the condition that the shadow from the building should never fall on his residence. Now, this aspect of the story is interpreted and retold many ways; the gist remains that Balu Nath wished to not be disturbed and left in peace.

However, later his warning was neglected and as the city grew bigger in population, the warning became a curse, and the entire city perished. There were mishaps and a lot of people died, and eventually the town was deserted.

Another telling of Bhangarh's haunting holds Rani Ratnavati (the former queen) accountable for the doom of the city. If legend is to be believed, Rani Ratnavati was extremely beautiful, and hence had a lot of admirers, from other states as well as within Bhangarh. One such admirer was a tantric named Singhia, who attempted to get the princess to fall in love with him by guileful means.

He disguised a potion laced with black magic that would make the princess infatuated with him, and gave it to one of her maids to give to her. The princess thwarted his plans by throwing away the bottle, which struck a boulder that starting rolling towards the tantric, trapping him under it and crushing him, eventually leading to his death. Before his demise, the tantric was said to have cursed the palace to its doom and the death of whoever resided in it.

The spooky part is not the black magic and the curses. It's what happened after. A year after the incident with Rani Ratnavati, it is said that Bhangarh was attacked, and that after the fierce battle that ensued, and ended with

Bhangarh losing, it has been uninhabited.

To this day, locals strongly believe in the paranormal presence residing within Bhangarh, and reports of spirits and ghost sightings come up every now and then.

Bachelor's Grove Cemetery

Any horror buff would immediately take a step back on hearing the word 'cemetery'. A place full of dead bodies can never be good, right?

Located in the outskirts of Chicago is the Bachelor's Grove cemetery, one of the scariest cemeteries worldwide. The cemetery is rather small and isolated, and in 1844, it was exclusively used for the burial of the immigrant community that resided close by.

Interesting rumours state that mobsters like Al Capone and other gangsters would often dispose of dead bodies by dumping them in the pond near the graveyard, though these rumours have never been confirmed.

One of the most popular ghost sightings in the Bachelor's Grove cemetery is that of a white lady, also called "White Madonna". This ghost appears as a lady holding an infant, and a photographed image of her even made it to the newspaper in 1991. Creepy? I think so too!

Other popular sightings in the area include a black dog, which witnesses claimed would disappear as they approached it, a glimmering farmhouse which would shrink and gradually disappear as one got closer, a farmer and his plough horse, both of whom had perished by being dragged to their deaths, a two headed ghost and a number of religious monks.

Evidence of erratic orbs has been found around the cemetery by ghost hunters, further solidifying the spooky nature and ghostly presence of this cemetery.

Lemp Mansion

Situated in St. Louis, this mansion housed John Adam Lemp who migrated from Germany in 1838. The family's fate was cursed, as Lemp Mansion witnessed a number of tragic incidents. The family suffered a bout of suicides and mysterious deaths.

John's son, William was the first to commit suicide in the family. In 1904, he killed himself after his son Frederick's death, which happened under mysterious circumstances. Followed by William's daughter Elsa who committed suicide in 1920, his son William Jr., who shot himself when their business failed to make profits and subsequently his other son Charles who also shot himself, in 1949, in the basement of the family home.

The only one to die a natural death was the youngest son who passed away in 1970, having instructed his caretaker to get rid of all their family heirlooms and destroy them. Following his demise, the house was sold and then converted to a hostel. Many of the boarders living in the house have complained of mysterious voices, and were scared to continue residing in the establishment.

According to the account of a woman who stayed overnight at the Lemp mansion, there was a loud and clearly discernible noise of ice being thrown into the sink, but on waking up and investigating the sink, there appeared to have been no such activity. Such accounts are narrated by a lot of visitors of the Lemp mansion.

One such account is that of Richard Pointer, or the Pointer family who purchased the mansion in 1975 to turn it into a restaurant. While painting the bathroom one day, Richard experienced unusual activity, and stated

"I was painting the bathroom by myself. There was no one else in the house, and I felt someone behind me, watching me. I mean, it was a terrible feeling, the most burning sensation you could have. I get goose bumps just now, thinking about it. I turned around, and nothing was there. I started working again and got the same feeling, so without looking behind me, I cleaned my paintbrushes and got the hell out of there."

Yet another such account is that of Claude Breckwoldt, a local painter, who says

"I was on the scaffolding, lying on my back and painting the ceiling in the dining room, when I got the feeling that someone was staring at me. I felt as though they were in the hallway just outside the room, but I couldn't see anything through the frosted glass doors. I went on working, and about an hour later, the feelings returned. It was weird. I felt like I just had to get out of there right then."

The Pointers have often complained of losing employees due to their experience of unusual happenings within the mansion. Ghost sightings are often the reason that employees decide to quit.

The Tower of London

The Tower of London has a history of the macabre that would make horror buffs clap their hands with glee. The history of The Tower of London is richly painted with torture and execution, making it one of the most haunted places in Britain.

Constructed originally in 1078, the Tower of London boasts of being a major part of England's cultural heritage. Of the many reports of paranormal happenings at the Tower, the most famous one would probably be that of the ghost of Anne Boleyn. The wife of King Henry VIII, Anne Boleyn was beheaded in 1536, after being charged with treason, adultery and incest. Often to this day, people have claimed to have seen her headless body walking the corridors of the Tower near the spot of her beheading.

A more mysterious and shudder inducing report is that of two children who have been seen throughout the castle, in various rooms. They are often reported to be sighted in their nightgowns, with looks of horror on their faces, whilst holding hands.

According to legend, these two are the ghosts of the illegitimate children bore by a former Prince, who was sent to the Tower and subsequently murdered one day by their uncle, and buried under a staircase in the Tower.

Other ghosts seen in the Tower include those of Lady Jane Grey, often spotted at the window in the White Tower where she once stood waving to her children.

Island of the Dolls – Xochimilco, Mexico

Chucky scares the hell out of me, and I think many would agree that although dolls are playthings, they are rather spooky. That being said, picture something called The Island of The Dolls. Scared yet? I know I am.

The island La Isla de la Munecas is situated on Lake Teshuilo in Xochimilco near Mexico City and is apparently dedicated to the lost soul of a young girl who met an early and sad demise under mysterious circumstances. It is said that in the 1920s, three little girls were playing near the water, when one of them fell in and drowned.

The legend of this island's haunting dates back to the 1950s, when a man called Julian Santan Barrera moved to the island and claimed that the spirit of this young girl would come and speak to him, telling him stories of her death, and how she was trapped on the island. This led Julian to buy dolls for the little girl to play with.

Julian spoke to his nephew a while later about how the girl's demands for these dolls was growing and could not be appeased, and how she wanted him to join her in her grave. The day Julian spoke to his nephew, his nephew was supposed to return to the island. On arriving, he found Julian in the same canal where the girl had died, with his face down.

The island is full of dolls, with their bodies dismembered and mutilated. According to some locals, Julian is said to have collected these dolls over 50 years of him staying on the island as a way of showing remorse over the girl's death. Locals claim that these dolls often move on their own accord, saying that they move their eyes and arms and heads, often whisper to each other and try to lure people into the water.

What can be scarier than visiting an island full of twisted dolls that move around and whisper to each other?

The Bedok Flats

Singapore follows a housing system where families reside in flats or apartments in tall buildings. A long time ago, in one of these flats, a strange and terrifying tragedy took place. This was near the Bedok Reservoir at Bedok North Avenue.

In one of these flats, lived a family of three; a man, his wife and child. Due to dwindling finances, the man took to gambling, in order to make some extra bucks. Subsequently, he got caught up in the vicious cycle of loan sharks and destroyed his family's finances altogether, leading to a lot of marital stress. After some time passed, the man got involved with a different woman and told his wife that he wanted a divorce. Struck by tragedy, the wife threw their three-year old child out of the window, before jumping 25 floors to meet her own death.

The story takes an interesting and spookier turn, however. Locals claim that after the demise of his wife and child, the man eventually went on to have a child with his mistress. On his second child's third birthday, the ghost of his firstborn convinced the child to leap off the balcony. As a result, the man's three year old child fell to his death, once again.

Different rumors suggest that yet another family had committed suicide in one of these flats, and that one person was found murdered in a freaky elevator accident.

People who live in the area claim that these flats are haunted. As a result, the apartments remain vacant due to the suspected paranormal activity there.

Changi Beach

War time stories are always interesting, and this one does not disappoint. During the Second World War, when the Japanese had occupied Singapore, their government wanted to rid the population of those who were anti-Japanese. So they set up centres for screening, where Japanese soldiers would round up all of Singapore's Chinese residents for execution. Anyone who they suspected of having anti-Japanese sentiments was a victim of this tyranny.

During these screenings, tens of thousands of residents were killed, the most famous of these centres being Changi beach. Suspects were shot and often beheaded.

Visitors of Changi beach today claim to hear wails of crying and loud screaming, and many are even reported to have seen dismembered heads floating in the air, or headless bodies roaming the beach. As per reports by visitors, the sand is often seen soaked in blood, and mass executions are often sighted too. What do you believe?

The Raynham Hall

The Brown Lady of Raynham Hall is one of the most popular ghost photographs of all time, and thus makes the Raynham Hall a force of paranormal activity to be reckoned with.

The Brown Lady, so named because of the brown brocade attire she appears in, is believed to be the ghost of Lady Dorothy Walpole, the second wife of Charles Townsend, and the sister of Sir Robert Walpole. The sightings of her ghost around the hall began shortly after her mysterious demise in 1726.

The reports of her ghost sighting have had some reputable sources, such as Major Loftus and Frederick Marryat, a friend of novelist Charles Dickens'. Loftus claims that as he was going to bed one night, a friend named Hawkins and he saw a woman in brown brocade that vanished as soon as he approached her. They saw the same apparition the next night and were duly horrified to notice that she had empty eye sockets.

Marryat's daughter writes of her father's experience in her account

"..He had his finger on the trigger of his revolver, and was about to demand it to stop and give the reason for its presence there, when the figure halted of its own accord before the door behind which he stood, and holding the lighted lamp she carried to her features, grinned in a malicious and diabolical manner at him. This act so infuriated my father, who was anything but

17

lamb-like in disposition, that he sprang into the corridor with a bound, and discharged the revolver right in her face. The figure instantly disappeared - the figure at which for several minutes' three men had been looking together and the bullet passed through the outer door of the room on the opposite side of the corridor, and lodged in the panel of the inner one. My father never attempted again to interfere with "The Brown Lady of Raynham"

The sightings of the Brown Lady came to prominence in 1936, when photographers from the magazine Country Life snapped a picture of the ghost transcending down the staircase of the hall. In the picture, the ghostly silhouette of a woman is very noticeably visible descending the stairs. Although the number of sightings have since then decreased, it still counts among one of the spookiest places in the country.

The Myrtle Plantation

No, this one is not about Moaning Myrtle from the Harry Potter novels, although it bears another connection to the books- a severed ear!

The Myrtle Plantation house located in St. Francisville, Louisiana, was constructed in 1796, and is widely regarded as one of the most eerie places in the United States, rumoured to be the site of ten murders. According to legend, a worker called Chloe had a penchant for eavesdropping, and on being caught in the act by her master one day, had her ear cut off by him. He forced her to wear a green scarf to cover her missing ear (a turban in other reports).

As revenge, she baked her master a cake and poisoned it with oleander leaves. Although her target was just the master, his daughters and wife ended up falling prey to her scheme instead. On hearing of their death, the other servants lynched and then hanged Chloe for her actions. It is said that Chloe haunts the estate, with the ghosts of her victims, and can often be spotted wearing the turban she used to cover her severed ear.

The Myrtle Plantation houses other ghosts as well, some of which include a young girl who chants voodoo over people and one who is often sighted in a mirror on the stairs. I have goose bumps already!

Hunedoara (Hunyad) Castle

Associated with the legend of Vlad the Impaler, the Hunedoara is regarded as one of the most terrifying castles of Europe. Situated in Russia, the Hunyad Castle has a large imposing size, which is attributed as the reason why the castle is still intact, while most other castles in the area were destroyed by invaders.

The Hunyad castle is over 13 storeys high, giving it its large imposing stature. On entering the yard, one can notice a well that is over 30 meters deep. According to local lore, twelve Turkish prisoners had dug the well as freedom was promised to them once they were able to find water. It took them fifteen years to dig the well, but the promise made by their captors was not kept, and they were beheaded. This disturbing piece of trivia about the castle adds to its spook value.

The castle is also the place where Vladimir the Impaler, the sadistic warlord, gained his hobby of impaling people. He soon became out of control and even started impaling the rats in his prison cell after being jailed by Janos Hunyadi. Vladimir sought to gain power by drinking the blood of his victims. Now if that doesn't sound macabre and horrifying to you, I don't know what does.

Residents of Transylvania are known to be superstitious people, and they believe in creatures they like to call Strigori. These creatures are known to be the souls of those rising from their graves, and possess the ability to shapeshift into an animal, to become invisible, and even drain the life of those they possess.

Strigori are said to affect those who have lived a life of sin, and once exposed, they would be cursed to wander the earth as the undead. To prevent Vladimir from returning as Strigori, locals tried to kill him by staking but eventually his grave was found empty, except for animal bones. What do you think happened to the crazy warlord?

The dark powers of the castle and the area around it are mystifying, and a force to be reckoned with. Would I stay the night here? Not even if you paid me.

Pluckley, Kent

St. Nicholas Church
Image Courtesy: Stephen Nunney (Wikimedia
Commons)

We often hear of the titles: "Scariest Places on Earth", "Most Haunted Locations", and "Spookiest Areas on the Planet", but seldom do websites announce -- officially -- which holds the No. 1 Spot.

And we cannot blame them, because quite honestly, it's hard to measure the "haunted-ness" of any area: while one group would attest that they have seen various apparitions, another group would offer the cold shoulder, insisting that there was nothing haunted about the place.

If you are looking for a certified, hands-down, MOST Haunted Place, then you must narrow down your choices; for instance, instead of saying "Scariest Place", why not say, "The Scariest *Village*"? And instead of saying "Most Haunted Villages in the World", why not turn it into: "The Most Haunted Village *in Britain*"?

This is exactly what we will discuss-- Britain's Most Haunted Village.

Pluckley, Kent in Britain

Many people describe Pluckley, Kent as a picturesque location; with merely one thousand residents, it's a little disturbing to accept that there is no "peace and quiet" in the village-- at least none in the *paranormal* sense.

Pluckley has been featured in countless TV shows, documentaries, and investigative series because it allegedly has at least 15 ghosts. In fact, it is so famous that police had no choice but to increase their presence during Halloween season because they expect ghoul seekers to invade the area.

Are you curious about these ghouls? Let's meet the 15 ghosts of Pluckley, Kent.

The Highwayman

It is believed that during the 18th century, an unnamed highwayman was killed after a fight happened between him and the lawmen. Allegedly, the lawmen pinned him on an oak tree before drawing a sword and killing him. Witnesses reported about seeing the "re-enactment" of the murder at the Fright Corner; so if ever you see one man getting attacked by a sword and being pinned on a tree, it might have been the murder of the 18th century highwayman.

The reason for the fight was never clarified, nor was the date of the killing, so it was hard to decipher if such an event really took place; for the witnesses though, the re-enactment was very real.

The Gypsy Woman

If you happen to reach Pinnock Bridge and see a misty figure sitting by the road, don't be surprised-- it could just be the ghost of the gypsy woman. Stories mention that this lady used to sell watercress (which she found on the stream) and that she died after being accidentally burnt.

Should you also see a womanly figure who is smoking, don't be fooled for it's still not a real person-- again, it is the gypsy lady; apparently some witnesses saw the apparition while it was smoking.

There's no telling what will happen if you approach this ghost because no reports were made about being in contact with it. Thus, if you saw the apparition and were brave enough to go near it or capture its attention, it would be nice if you could blog about the experience!

Lost in Time

Down in Maltman's Hill, a carriage seems to be lost in time. Several accounts mentioned something about seeing a horse-drawn coach down the street. One of the accounts came from a babysitter who related that once, while she was walking home, she saw a carriage being pulled by a horse; she also added that the windows of the coach were filled with inexplicable light.

But, hold your horses and don't immediately proceed to Maltman's Hill! Reports indicated that even though most manifestations happen in that area, the carriage could be seen anywhere in Pluckley-- as if it is lost or is purposely traveling. In fact, in 1997, a person who was driving around the village suddenly heard "horses hooves on cobbles inside their car".

The Suicide Men

Shortly after World War I, a teacher, particularly a headmaster, had gone missing. Weeks went by and people had no idea where he was until a miller, Dicky Buss, found his dangling corpse. It was said that to this day, the dangling corpse of the headmaster can still be seen, right at the spot where he was found (which is now interestingly called, Dicky Buss Lane).

Aside from the teacher, another suicide victim resides in Pluckley-- he is unnamed, but people knew him to be a colonel. Reports said he hanged himself in Park Wood, but unlike the headmaster, it isn't his hanging body that makes an appearance-- he is said to be walking through the trees.

To date, the park has been cleared of trees, but it doesn't stop the colonel from showing himself.

Dicky Buss

Believe it or not, but Dicky Buss, the man who found the body of the headmaster, is also haunting the village. Dicky, whose real name was Richard, allegedly visits the windmill near the house called *The Pinnock* whenever a thunderstorm is coming. Stories have it that he closed the mill down during the 1930s and that it had been destroyed by fire (after lighting hit it) in the year 1939.

Perhaps this is the reason why Dicky roams the area every time a thunderstorm is approaching: he wanted to guard the ruins of the mill he loved the most against the lightning that ultimately destroyed it.

Terror at Brickworks

Inside the village, you will find a modern-day brickworks building; but no matter how modern it looks, the past still catches up to it.

Apparently, in the past, one worker had been killed in the building after a wall of clay fell on him; the man died, but not before screaming for help and shouting from pain. As of now, residents of the area still hear his scream shortly before his death.

Paranormal in the Pub

If you are looking for the most haunted place in Pluckley, residents will point you to Blacksmith's Arms Pub. Its reputation as a haunted place is so extensive that in the past, it had been called "The Spectre's Arms" and "The Ghost's Arms".

Your chances of seeing a ghost here are high, considering the number of spirit patrons existing inside, including a Tudor maid, a Cavalier who has a habit of roaming the second floor rooms, and a coachman, who appears to be always looking at the fire by the public lounge.

If you were unlucky and didn't see anything, then you could still enjoy the food, the drinks, and the ambiance!

The Dering Arms

If you have no chance encounter with a ghost at the Blacksmith's Arms, why not proceed to the Dering's Arms? While it holds just one ghost, patrons swear that she is pretty active and very life-like.

Dering Arms was said to be an old haunted lodge before it was turned into a pub; since the transformation, an old-lady wearing a bonnet became a regular "customer"-- those who had an encounter with her said that she mixes in the crowd. Her presence is so normal that patrons often mistake her for a real human.

At the Black Horse

Still no luck with the Black Arms? Why not visit the Black Horse Pub? Here, people don't often *see* ghosts, but they lose personal belongings without any reason at all. The items missing (usually extra clothes) will turn up several days later, out of nowhere, and in places they have looked at previously.

As to who could be "borrowing" these items, the residents have no answer yet-- all they know is that the building was once a farmhouse surrounded by a moat and that a bailiff once resided there.

Once in the pub, make sure that you keep an eye on your important belongings-- sure, the ghost has a habit of returning the items, but it will be inconvenient for you to retrieve it, especially if you are a tourist!

The Red and the White Ladies

The St. Nicholas Church in Pluckley had a crypt (area underneath where tombs are kept), and back in the 1100s, a Lady Hering was buried there. After her burial, many residents saw her roaming the grounds of the church; they believed that she rose from her grave to look for her stillborn baby. People began calling her "The Red Lady" due to the red rose petals scattered on the top of her coffin. Walk around the church and you might just see her.

If not the Red Lady, then perhaps the White Lady will grace you with her presence. The white apparition was also another Dering Lady and she is seen haunting not just the grounds of the church, but also her previous home (Surrenden Dering) which was destroyed by fire in the year 1952.

During the two World Wars, the Surrenden Dering was used by the US Embassy employees and many of them conveyed on seeing the white apparition. In fact, a man (who only went by the name "Mr. Walter") spent the night alone in the library of the house during one Christmas Eve.

While resting, the White Lady appeared in front of him -- in his fear, he took his shotgun and fired at her, only to have the bullet pass through the spirit.

The Monk

The Greystone is an antic house in Pluckley; it was built in 1863 and first went by the name of Rectory Cottage-- a house meant to accommodate the curator of St. Nicholas Church. Here, the spirit of a monk was said to roam the area until the year 1924, when the name was changed from Rectory House to Greystone.

Residents said that since the change of name happened, the monk stopped showing himself-- or perhaps, he still does, only, not when someone is looking.

The Poisoned Tudor Lady

For the past 250 years, Rose Court had been the dwelling of the spirit of a Tudor Lady. Residents believe that she killed herself after finding a handful of poisonous berries and eating them all. Her identity was never disclosed, but many believed her to be a mistress of a Dering man. At around 4:00 pm or 5:00 pm, she would be heard shouting for her two dogs-- this time frame was said to be her hour of death.

Aren't you intrigued? A village like Pluckley, which has a lot of history-rich areas, will surely cause some form of haunting. Ghost seekers should definitely put it on top of their "to go to" list.

Hill of Cross

Image Courtesy: Diego Delso (Wikimedia Commons)

Some people create a "vision board" for them to keep track of their success-- this is where they may write their desires, post cutout pictures of their "dream" things, or paste little memorabilia to remind them of happy times. Most people use a simple cardboard for this, if that's too big, then a folder-size notebook will do.

Imagine if you have a board as big as a hill, but the contents are not about happy memories and aspirations. What it contains are hundreds of thousands of crosses, each holding a sad, bitter story.

One Lithuanian Hill

Just outside the city of Šiauliai, in the green ambiance of Lithuanian Countryside, sits a mystery for tourists: a hill filled with hundreds of thousands of crosses in a snake-form arrangement.

Some of the crucifixes are big, some are small; many of the minute ones are placed on top of the bigger ones in an organized (but chaotic-looking) fashion. Many crosses are made of wood, some are made of metal, and others are made of granite-- due to this, their appearance seem "messy" and tourists can't help but question their purpose.

As they near the infamous Hill of Crosses, however, the passion of the crucifixes are revealed. Many crosses have flowers around them, many too, hold Rosaries, as if to say that it was an offering to a lost loved one.

Each has a story to tell

No one knows for certain when the custom of leaving a cross at the hill started; people only knew that the place (which is mysterious on its own), once held a fort. Their suspicion was that in the year 1831, the first bitter cross was erected there, and soon enough, other people who also wanted to release some grief, followed the act.

Why 1831?

Apparently, this year marked the end of the November Uprising-- the movement initiated by Poland in 1830 which aimed to help them break free from the Russian hold. In this uprising, other neighboring countries (which were also controlled by Russia) also joined, namely: Western Belarus, several parts of Ukraine and of course, Lithuania.

Even though they got a lot of support, their army only

reached one third of the total number of the Russian soldiers. The end of the war was bittersweet-- true, they lost the battle and freedom was not obtained, but the good thing was, deaths would also stop.

The November Uprising left at least 40,000 deaths. The families of the fallen probably left crosses on the hill because they were not able to recover the dead bodies. They chose the hill because it was where the fort was located.

In 1863, with the people from controlled countries still hungry for freedom, another uprising began-- it was named January Uprising. Aside from the above mentioned countries, people from Latvia and Western Russia also offered their support to the oppressed, letting them gain more leverage. However, through the years, Russia's army also became stronger, hence the battle's result was another victory for Russia.

This time between 10,000 to 20,000 people died. Similar to the postwar period of November Uprising, many bodies were not retrieved, so families placed crosses on the hill once more as a sign of grief, sadness, and loss.

After the First World War, Lithuania fought three more battles for their freedom, resulting to three other bouts of tragic deaths. From only hundreds of crosses in the year 1938, it grew to thousands in the 1960s, even when the hill was bulldozed three times between 1961 and 1975. Some of the crosses disappeared after the bulldozing, but the next day, they would be replaced, and soon enough, other crosses were added.

In the year 1990, the number of crosses was said to have reached 55,000. This was largely due to the presence of miniature crucifixes draped on the larger ones. People surmised that the number grew drastically in that year because it was the period when Lithuania finally obtained their independence, hence, many citizens showed their thanks and support to the fallen by offering a cross for them. In time, even international communities started admiring this act of spirituality.

Many tourists visit the hill, not only because they want a glimpse of Lithuanian solidarity, but also because they want to see something haunted.

The Hill of Crosses is Haunted

Unlike other haunted locations, the Hill of Crosses offers very few ghostly tales. The apparitions, disembodied voices, and weird sounds might have come from the connection between the fallen insurgents and the cross which represented them.

Searching the internet about "spooky places" and "haunted locations" will truly bring you to Lithuania's sacred hill, but seldom would you find accounts which state an actual, face-to-face experience with a ghost. All there is, is heavy feelings of depression, feelings of being watched, and unexplained appearances of shadow figures.

To make things more interesting, people also claim that the Hill is where Christ performs his miracles, particularly curing the sick. This is emphasized by the fact that annually, pilgrims from all over the world come to the area to ask for healing. While offering their prayer, the pilgrims take a cross, and place it there. This is why the number of crosses continues to grow year after year.

When Lithuanian people were asked where the idea came from, they said it was from a legend, which, interestingly, also explained the appearance of the first cross on the hill.

According to the legend, there was once a farmer whose daughter was gravely ill-- she was examined by every doctor, but none of them could offer any medication or treatment regimen which could alleviate the girl's suffering; if any, her situation only got worse. Finding out that he could do nothing else, the farmer sat by her bed and prayed every night.

The prayers were unanswered until one night, when a lady in white approached him in his dreams. The lady said that his daughter would recover if he would follow her instructions, which only stated that he should build a large wooden cross and place it at the hill where the Domantai Fort was. The lady added that the cross was a sign of faith, and that in faith, there is healing.

Relieved for something that he could do, the father set out and built the cross. After it was placed on the hill, his daughter miraculously got better. While not many would believe this legend (as they prefer to believe *the cross for the insurgents* theory), it is obvious that people have already associated the lady in white as Mother Mary, hence, some parts of the cross-laden hill are also filled with images of Christ's Mother.

Whatever the case may be, paranormal enthusiasts who have visited the place and were not able to witness anything ghostly were still embraced by the overwhelming presence of more than 400,000 pieces of crosses, each symbolizing a story of sadness, remembrance, and gratefulness.

Toni Jo's Haunting at Calcasieu Parish Courthouse

Annie Beatrice McQuiston, a woman who was more famous by her name, Toni Jo Henry, was the first female killer in the state of Louisiana. Worse, she was only 26 years old when she was executed in the electric chair.

Toni Jo was not just beautiful, she was also intelligent; however, her ugly past hindered her from having a fulfilling life. At a young age of only 4, Toni Jo's mother died, forcing her aunt to take her in. The household was dysfunctional in every sense as Toni Jo was not just unloved, she was also neglected.

Sure, she was sent to school, but no one at home supervised her progress for nobody cared, soon enough, she got tired of having a bad life at home and at school, so at the age of 13, she ran away. Toni Jo desired to start fresh, but the road to it would be difficult and tragic, especially since she was not even a grade school finisher.

Soon after leaving, Toni Jo became widely known in her hometown in Lake Charles, Louisiana as a "lewd woman", which, in context, meant she was immoral and obscene. This was probably because of the fact that she was addicted to cocaine and that she worked in a brothel as a prostitute-- and she was only 17 years old!

Throughout the years, Toni Jo was arrested for various offenses, including vagrancy (being a drifter), larceny (stealing someone's personal property), and hurting someone, by almost cutting off his ear. Before long, people started calling her "the most ornery gal east of the Mississippi".

All in all, Toni Jo's life was a mess-- she was an addict, a prostitute, a drifter, and she seemed to have let go of any form of human connection: there was no family and friends to care for her and people only saw her as a bad influence-- someone whom parents would protect their children from. All this changed when Toni Jo met the man of her life-- Claude Henry.

The Cowboy

Texan guy Claude Henry, more known as "Cowboy", met 23-year old Toni Jo in 1939 at the brothel where she worked. After meeting each other, the two hit it off right away. Claude was a good influence to the sidetracked Toni Jo and he was even able to curb her addiction to cocaine.

They were in love, and in an instant, they were married. Everything was finally falling into place-- they even had their honeymoon in California and were set to start a family, with Toni Jo probably promising to become a good wife and in the future, a better mother.

But then, Claude's past haunted him.

As soon as they arrived in Louisiana, Claude was arrested-- apparently, before they met, he had killed a police officer in Texas and had been a fugitive since. Because of this, he was taken back to Texas to be tried, leaving Toni Jo, his new wife, hopeless. After the trial, it was decided that for his crime, Claude "Cowboy" Henry was to spend 50 years in prison at Texas State Penitentiary in Huntsville.

Without her man, the new bride was restless; she easily fell back into her old ways of drugs and booze, until finally, she decided on something that would change (and end) her life.

Toni Jo planned on going to Texas and breaking Claude out of the prison and because it was a pretty hard task, she consulted an accomplice, Harold Finnan Burks, better known as "Arkie". The two of them didn't have a solid plan; in fact, they schemed to reach Texas only through hitchhiking rides from other motorists. With that said, it was obviously a disaster waiting to happen.

And it did happen.

Toni Jo, Louisiana's First Female Killer

Outside Lake Charles, a car salesman by the name of Joseph P. Calloway (Note: In some reports, his surname was Crowley) offered to give them a ride. Instead of just taking the offer, Arkie and Toni Jo plotted to "get rid" of him because they thought that his Ford V8 coupe was the perfect escape vehicle after getting Claude out of prison.

With this plan in mind, they asked Joseph to pull over when they reached Jennings, a small town nearby. After stopping the vehicle, Joseph was commanded to get out and strip, then he was tortured. Finally, Toni Jo asked him to "say his prayers" before she grabbed a pistol and shot him between the eyes, instantly killing him. They then left Joseph's body in a ditch.

Perhaps thinking that their crime was an accomplishment, the two drove the Ford and went to a roadhouse to get drunk. When the liquor went to their head, their mouths became unstoppable-- they literally bragged about the murder they committed. Soon enough, the two were arrested and Joseph's body was found.

Mission Unaccomplished

In other words, the two didn't even reach the prison in Huntsville, for they were taken into custody and were tried for the murder of Joseph Calloway at the Calcasieu Parish Courthouse, where, during Toni Jo's first trial, more than a hundred people gathered and shouted "Hang her, hang her!"

Arkie denied that he pulled the trigger, insisting that it was Toni Jo who did it, and he was just there to help with the plan to break Claude out of prison. Toni Jo, on the other hand, claimed that it was Arkie who killed Joseph and that she just stood and watched in horror. This back and forth blaming only caused the court to have them both executed-- on March of 1940, Annie Beatrice McQuiston Henry was sentenced to death.

In the Parish Courthouse, Toni Jo was treated as a celebrity-- she was allowed to keep a pet and a hairdresser, not the prison barber, cut her hair. Under close supervision, Claude even visited her and that was when Toni Jo admitted to the crime, telling her husband that she shot Joseph "right between the eyes".

A second and a third trial was performed, but the result didn't change. A fourth trial was denied because it was as if the defense team would use the ever-famous insanity plea. The schedule of the execution was on November 28, 1942 and since Louisiana changed their execution method, Toni Jo would have to endure the pain of sitting in an electric chair instead of being hanged.

When Claude heard of this, he tried to escape the prison to save his wife, but was also recaptured quickly.

Toni Jo's dying wish was to see Claude Henry and talk to him one last time, and although it was supposed to be forbidden, her request was granted. Reports said Toni Jo talked while Claude only cried. She also wrote two letters-- one was for Claude, telling him how much she loved him, and one was for the court, a formal admittance that it was her and not Arkie who killed Joseph. Despite her attempt to right the wrong, Arkie was still executed.

Since her execution, Toni Jo haunted the Calcasieu Parish Courthouse.

Manifestations

People who work at the courthouse report on hearing footsteps; they also get a whiff of a perfume that could have only been made during the 1940s. From time to time, a woman would also speak out of the blue, but no one could pinpoint the exact message of the ghost.

Inside the courthouse was a rotating file system, which could only be turned on and off using a key; accounts said that when no one was near the file, it would magically turn off by itself-- they believe it to be the workings of Toni Jo Henry.

At the stairs near the area of her execution, a shrill scream of a woman could also be heard.

Tony Jo Henry's story could have ended differently had she just waited; apparently, just a few years after her execution, Claude was released from prison. However, within ten years, he was also shot to death.

The murder she committed was senseless in all aspects; had they simply took Joseph's ride offer and not killed him, perhaps, she and Claude would be able to spend their lives together.

Forepaugh's Restaurant in Minnesota

Image Courtesy: Elkman (Wikimedia Commons)

East of Irvine Park, on South Exchange Street and Walnut, sits a magnificent manor turned French Restaurant, the Forepaugh's. The building is a Victorian-style mansion with a very accommodating banquet/reception hall. It has three floors, with a basement and a ballroom area.

Aside from providing people with a glimpse of wealth, Forepaugh's Restaurant also offers authentic French cuisine, they host parties like wedding and birthdays, and they give a slight twist of haunting to your dining experience.

History

Forepaugh's Manor was built by Joseph Lybrandt Forepough, a successful entrepreneur who made fortunes out of his dry-goods business. Aside from that, he was also a senior partner at J.L. Forepaugh and Company.

When the time was right, Joseph bought 5 lots and in the center, he built a mansion with a basement, three floors, and intricately designed furnishing. On top of that, it also had a perfectly landscaped garden which was perfect for a banquet. After the mansion had been completed, Joseph's wife, Mary, and their two daughters moved in.

With such a great manor, Joseph needed people to help him and his wife take care of the chores, so he hired several housemaids. One of those maids was a woman named Molly, whom Joseph developed an affair with. When Mary discovered the affair (she caught them in bed), she insisted that Joseph should end it right then and there.

Realizing that it was the right thing to do, Joseph finished his illicit relationship with the poor housemaid who was already pregnant at that point. Desperate and confused, Molly did the only thing she could think of: she took a long rope, tied the first end to the chandelier, tied the second end to her neck, and threw herself out of the window. The year it happened was said to be 1865.

In 1866, Joseph decided to rekindle his relationship with his wife (and forget about Molly), so they moved out of the house and moved to Europe. In the process, he sold the Forepaugh's Manor to Civil War veteran, John Henry Hammond. They came back 3 years later and built another mansion-like house at Summit Avenue, which offered a great view of their previous manor.

However, things were not getting better; if any, it got worse.

In 1992, Joseph got extremely depressed, he claimed that he was worried about his business, but the truth was, he still couldn't get over Molly's death. One day, he went to the park and shot himself dead.

Through the years, the luxurious mansion had transferred ownership multiple times and since money was needed to keep it well-furnished, the current owner turned it into a French Restaurant.

Manifestations

It is believed that Molly and Joseph still roam the mansion up to this day. Many restaurant staff and customers have seen them, especially Joseph in his 1890s clothes. Witnesses say whenever he shows up, he appears to be looking pleased-- as if he approved of the renovations done to the mansion he previously owned. Some customers even mentioned that he walked like the master of the house, as if it is still his!

Down in the basement, various accounts indicate that the lights turn on and off by themselves, staff would suddenly feel cold, and they would hear weird noises.

Molly, on the other hand, had been seen multiple times near the area where she killed herself. Once too, when there was a 19th century themed reception (where staff and waitresses wore 19th century clothes), a woman who also wore 19th century clothing, but was different from the staff, glided through the hall before it melted into the wall.

Once, when the staff were opening the restaurant, they heard a very clear tromping sound on the third floor. Afraid that there were burglars, they called the police who even brought a dog. The dog refused to investigate the third floor, but after some coaxing, he went upstairs-- the sound stopped but they never saw anyone who could have done the tromping.

Rumors have it that Molly was a "sociable ghost", that most of the time, she would be present at certain events like weddings, birthdays, and banquets. In fact, there was an instance when her image was captured in one of the wedding photos.

Many assume that Molly and Joseph haunt the basement of the manor and that it is their rendezvous point, allowing them the fulfillment of their desire to be together even after death. This might be true, for in their previous life, they had not been careful enough, that's why Mary caught them; perhaps now, they chose the basement for it is hidden from prying eyes. Good thing Mary is still not making an appearance...

Haunted M6 Motorway

Image Courtesy: Phillip Capper (Wikimedia Commons)

Aside from houses, hotels, and restaurants, roads can also be haunted. One such road is the M6 located in Sandbach (Route 17), Cheshire, England. People who are unfamiliar with the road would love to drive on it-- it is a perfectly straight road with little distractions on the side, giving any driver the needed concentration for safe journey.

One should feel safe when traveling on it, since it is one of the busiest roads in Britain, and is in fact, considered as Britain's backbone; however, traffic reports reveal that many accidents happen in the area. Why is that so?

Apparently, the M6 Motorway is haunted (#18 Most Haunted Roads in the World according to www.dangerousroads.org). Motorists could get distracted not by physical things, but by ghosts.

According to stories, the abandoned Saxon Cross Hotel, which is just off the M6 road, was once occupied by the

Scottish Army after they retreated from the Battle of Worcester in 1651. In the middle of their rest, they were attacked by the locals of Sandbach. Since then, shadows can be seen along the road.

A Bagpiper has also been seen haunting the area, but no one knew for certain who he was and why he was haunting the place. Sometimes, too, he would not manifest, but a bagpipe could be heard playing in the spot where he was witnessed by others.

The number of Scottish soldiers who died in the fight was hard to determine, some reports said there were only 10, while others say there was more. Still, being killed brutally is a very valid reason for a person to haunt the place, as he (or she) was unprepared for the departure, let alone, a violent one.

People who have not seen ghosts still find the road strange considering the amount of accidents happening in the area. One account claimed that once, there were three accidents in three consecutive days and at least three died.

One witness saw the first accident and she said that the lorry (big vehicle for transporting goods) just "pulled to the side and backed for no reason", hitting 2 pedestrians in the process. People assumed that the driver saw something that made him pull back.

In another incidence, a truck driver, together with a coworker, was driving along M6, when all of a sudden "a man who was wearing clothes from hundreds of years ago" popped out of nowhere. He tried to swerve to the side to avoid the man, but both of them witnessed the man pass through their truck.

Scared that he had killed someone, the driver stopped the vehicle and checked outside, but no one was there. When he went home, he kept vigil on the news just in case a body on the road turned up, but after days of watching TV, he accepted that they had hit no one-- at least not a normal person.

One account posted by someone named Catherine, related an event that happened in 1983, concerning her parents. According to her, her parents were travelling from their home in Lancaster to some relatives in Bedfordshire. While driving the M6, they saw a completely burnt out car which was stationary; when they passed by it, they were horrified to note that there was an elderly couple in the driver's seat and passenger's seat. Worse, they were wearing clothes from the 1960s! Aside from them, others too have experienced this sighting.

Near the M6, at Junction 16, one spooky incident also took place. According to a poster, who worked as a traffic bobby in the area, they had received many reports from motorists about a hitchhiker who frequently thumbed a lift; he was described as a biker for he wore an open-face helmet, goggles, long coat, and gauntlet gloves.

They attended to these reports multiple times, but never saw the infamous hitchhiker. However, they knew that, years before the reports started pouring in, police had found a classic bike leaning against one of the barriers with no motorist around. They waited if anyone would claim the bike, but no one did.

Years after that, people who were cleaning the undergrowth below the barrier finally found who could be the driver of the motorbike: a man wearing a long coat, helmet, goggles, and gauntlet gloves was slumped in the area. Police suspected that his bike hit the barrier and he was thrown into the undergrowth, making it hard for the authorities to find him.

In one incidence, a man came running to the police, pale and visibly shaken. In his account, he said that he offered a ride to a hitchhiker, but when he turned to ask where he would like to be dropped off, the hitchhiker was gone.

Because of the haunting experiences of motorists on the M6, many try to avoid the road as much as they can. If they could journey through a different road, then they would, if not, they would simply abide by the golden rule: never pick up a hitchhiker, especially one that looked suspicious or one that came out of nowhere, because most likely, it is a ghost!

Chapter 2:

Ghost Stories from Haunted Forests

Something about dense shrubbery, tall, thick trees, the rustling of leaves in the night accompanied with the sound of strong, gushing wind, creeps me out instantly. No matter how brave or how much of a non-believer in ghosts one is, I doubt many people would opt to stay overnight in a dense, haunted forest just for kicks.

Who knows what horrors its dense foliage may hold? And when the forests are like the ones in this section, you might just want to take a step back- or a hundred.

Screaming Woods

The Dering Woods or as they more commonly known, Screaming Woods are situated south of Pluckley, Britain. Pluckley in itself has the reputation of being one of the most haunted villages in Britain, and the Screaming Woods add to its ghostly allure.

The woods are said to have derived their name due to the blood curdling screams reported to have been heard from the forest late in the night. The haunting of the woods can be attributed to a highwayman who was captured by the villagers, pinned to the tree and murdered with a sword, and is said to haunt the woods along with a man who fell to his death, screaming. One visitor recounts-

"I was in Pluckley and a group of friends and I decided to go to Dering woods. When we got there, there were birds singing and the atmosphere seemed quite happy. As we pulled up and got out of the car, my friend and I noticed that the birds had stopped singing. As we went into the woods, you could have heard a pin drop. We walked in up to half way towards the cross roads and us girls decided to come out, so we went into the car and the boys went back in. About 20 minutes later the boys came running out. They got in the car, started the car and turned it head on to the woods where my friend's brand new car stalled head on and we saw this dark black mist coming towards us as if it was walking down the path. We then went down to the black horse pub where we discussed the day's ghost hunt as we always did and the boys said that it was only when they started getting close

to the crossroads that the mist appeared so they ran out. We have spoken to a few of the local people, who have said that early in the morning you can hear screaming coming from the woods."

Aokigahara Forest

I don't need to stress on how macabre this forest is- it literally is known as the "Death Forest" or the "Suicide Forest". Aokigahara or Sea of Trees is a forest spanning across 35 square kilometres, at the north-west base of Mount Fuji, Japan. The forest is so dense, that one may wander through it in the daytime, in pitch darkness. Crazy, right? The forest is also remarkably quiet, as the density of the forest blocks the wind, and there is a stark absence of wildlife.

According to Japanese mythology, this forest is well known for having demonic associations- a large one at that. The reason the forest is known as Death Forest is because it is the second most popular site for suicides. Owing to the dense nature of the forest, the Japanese authorities sometimes have intense trouble removing the bodies of those who wandered the forests to never return again.

The suicides in the forests are said to have started as a trend following Seicho Matsumoto's novel, Kuroi Kaiju aka the Black Sea of Trees wherein two of his characters kill themselves in the Aokigahara forest. Paranormal activity resulting from the suicides is also held accountable for the deaths of people who enter the forest's depths, prohibiting them from leaving.

Dow Hill

Dow Hill, situated in Kurseong, West Bengal, India is a destination most people would prefer to keep a safe distance from. Paranormal activity is often reported around the area, and it is said that the spirits wreaking havoc, reside in the Victorian Boys High School.

There have been reports of footsteps being heard in the hallways of the school during vacations. Adding to the sinister feel of the school are reports that say that people have heard boys laughing and running in the corridors of the building- when empty.

In the woods, a lot of murders have been committed, and the ghost of one young headless boy is said to haunt the roads. According to local myth, those who see the ghost of the headless boy will end up being haunted by him forever. The whole area has an unsettling vibe to it, and people who visit the place are often affected by the spirits even long after they have left the place.

Ballyboley Forest

Located in Larne, Northern Ireland, the Ballyboley forest is sinister and chill inducing. Local legends claim that the forest was a Druid site in ancient times, or a getaway to "The Otherworld", as per Celtic lore. The legends arise from the circular trenches and stone formations that give the Ballyboley forest its remarkable appearance.

The locals in Northern Ireland wouldn't dare step foot into the Ballyboley forest; that is how strongly they believe in the mystical and paranormal aura of the forest. According to legends associated with the forest, it is haunted by figures that look like humans, dressed in brown rags.

Screams of moaning women have been heard, along with sightings of blood-smeared trees and columns of black smoke. Shadowy figures of both humans and animals are reported to walk through the forests late at night.

It is also rumoured that between the 15th and 17th centuries, people wandered into the forest- never to return.

Epping Forest

The Epping Forest in Essex, England has a link with crime, making it all the more fascinating to read about. The popular highway man Dick Turpin is said to have had a hideout in the woods, which he lived in for many years in the High Beach area of the forest. Here, Dick Turpin, along with his partner Tom King would jump travellers and rob them at gunpoint. The ghost of Dick Turpin is said to still haunt the woods.

Because of how close the forest is to London, it has often served as a burial site in the past, for murder victims. Apparitions have been reported in the forest, such as sightings of these murder victims. There even is a morbid spot called Hangman's Hill at High Beach, where cars go uphill even when put in neutral. Such claims were falsified as optical illusions, till people tested it to see whether it was an optical illusion. Turns out, it's not an optical illusion after all.

A different story related to Epping Forest dates back almost 300 years and tells the story of a young couple that died in the forest. As the story goes, the young couple met each other near a pool in the forest, when the girl's father saw them and killed her next to the pool in a fit of rage, as he disapproved of the relationship.

Her lover was so upset that he killed himself at the exact spot where his girlfriend was murdered. After this incident, the water of the pool is reported to have turned black, and no wildlife could ever approach it. Gaining popularity as a suicide pool with some dark powers, the eeriest part about it is that it has never been located.

Chapter 3:

Mysterious and Spooky Incidents

Unexplained mysteries, or spooky happening are a personal favourite of mine to read about. How else do you explain the apparition of a woman engulfed in flames, resembling a ball of fire, materializing in front of a train only to vanish moments later? The paranormal, of course. This section focuses on freak incidents, mishaps and mysterious stories that are bound to send a chill down your spine.

The Dyatlov Pass Incident

Hiking and skiing are regular and popular hobbies, right? So obviously, it wasn't surprising when a group of experienced hikers went on a skiing trip in Russia, in the winter of 1959. However, the story gets spooky when they went missing.

Their camp was found eventually – and of the many horrifying things that stood out, the first and most noticeable one was that all the hikers (now dead) were wearing very little clothing, which was unnerving, given the place and season. The bodies of the first two hikers recovered, were reported as having been shoeless and only in their underwear. Not only this, their tents appeared to be ripped open from the inside.

This wasn't the worst of it. While there were no signs of struggle, the doctor associated with the incident reported that the extent of the injuries they sustained resembled that of a car crash, and left the bodies of the victims stained orange. The hikers were found with their skulls fractured, ribs broken and one woman was found with her tongue, eyes, and some other parts of her face - missing.

Three of the corpses are said to have been found in positions that suggest they were trying to return to the tent. Journalists report that the inquest files claim that six members of the group succumbed to hypothermia and passed away, while three others died of fatal injuries.

The final report says that the hikers died due to a "compelling natural force" but that just sounds like a clever cover-up, right? The entire incident is vague and ambiguous and has been left open for interpretation for those who do not buy into the "force of nature" spiel.

Calls from the Dead

Charles E. Peck was one of the passengers of a train that would take him from Salt Lake City to Los Angeles for a job interview. He was optimistic about it as well – as it meant he would be moving closer to his fiancée, Andrea Katz, who lived in California. Even better was the fact that the two were going to get married if he was hired.

However, fate had different plans for him – and the train he was travelling by was one of the two trains that collided in Chatsworth district, Los Angeles, on 12th September, 2008. 25 people were killed in the crash. However, Charles' brother, his son, fiancée, stepmother and sister received several calls from him over the next half of the day, a whooping number of 35 calls in all!

This led all of them to believe he was alive: after all, they could only hear static, and if they did try to call back, the call went to voicemail. This probably meant he had somehow survived and needed help.

Finally, a search team discovered Peck's body in one of the passenger cars in the front, where most deaths were observed, and most injuries were sustained. They realized that Charles could not have made any of those calls, as he died on impact from the collision.

Furthermore, they never did find the phone.

Resurrection Mary

Resurrection Mary is one of best known stories related to ghost sightings at night. It all began in Chicago, Illinois, around the 1930s, when a motorist reported that he saw a woman dressed in white along Archer Avenue. More and more reports emerged of a young woman who would always be dressed in white, and would be standing in front the Resurrection Cemetery. Several people also mentioned she would try to get a ride from a running car.

As the reports increased in number, people began noticing her away from the cemetery as well. Some young men also found her walking close to O'Henry ballroom – some even said they had danced with her. They would offer to drop her home, but she would disappear as soon as they got close to the cemetery gates.

Another series of reports claims that people would offer her a ride, and she would get in the car, only to disappear while in the car, or close to the cemetery. All these accounts have one thing in common – the description of the young woman is the same, as is the description of the clothes she was wearing.

There are two stories surrounding Resurrection Mary. One claims she was a young woman who had stormed out of O'Henry ballroom, and died in a hit and run. The other story claims she was returning from a funeral when she was run over by a car.

Robert the Haunted Doll

We've all heard about ghosts possessing people – but dolls, that's just taking it to a whole new level! Something of this sort happened in Key West, Florida, in the year 1897. The Otto family owned a plantation in this area. One day Robert Eugene Otto, the son of Mr. Otto was gifted a doll by one of the servant girls in the plantation – a doll that many believed was cursed with voodoo magic (Local historians believe the girl might have been practicing voodoo.)

Once the doll was brought into the house, the neighbors sighted it moving from one window to another, even when there was nobody at home. Not only this, the family themselves could hear the doll at night, giggling and running around. It caused chaos in the house to the point that it even ransacked the little boy's bedroom.

However, Robert did not part with the doll even then. As he grew up, he kept the doll with him, and often isolated himself in his room for hours talking to the doll. He had the doll even after he got married to a woman named Anne, who despised the doll. She eventually forced him to keep it in the attic, and he listened, but not for long, and brought it back to a room with a window. Yet again, the sightings of the doll moving emerged.

It might be said now that Robert was the one who was insane. However, this idea was disproved after Robert died, and Anne left the home. She leased it on the condition that the doll (named Robert) remained in the attic. Families too, began hearing the doll run around in the attic and discovered its position changed the next morning. The giggling that the Otto family heard didn't stop either.

When Anne died, the doll was placed in the East Martello Museum after finally being separated from the house, where several reports of strange, unexplainable activity still emerge, surrounding the doll.

Telly Savalas and the Good Samaritan

It seems like ghosts can be helpful too, as discovered by the encounter Telly Savalas, the Kojack actor, had in 1959. Telly was returning to Long Island after a date, late in the night, when he ran out of gas. Left with no choice, he started walking towards the freeway when he heard a high-pitched voice behind him that offered to give him a ride. He hadn't heard the car, but he did see the man in the white suit driving the Cadillac.

They travelled to the gas station together, where the man bought Savalas what he needed. Savalas, on his part, noted down the man's name and address, so he could repay the man back the next day. Then, while driving Savalas back to his car, the man told him how he knew a Red Sox basketball player, even giving him the name. The man helped Savalas fill his car with gas and pushed it to get the car started while Savalas took the wheel.

The very next day, the newspaper headlines reported the death of the same Red Sox player that the man had named as his contact. This is where things take a turn for the utterly eerie. Perplexed, Savalas called the number that the man had given him, and spoke with a woman who picked up. She continued to get irritated with their conversation, telling him that her husband had been dead for over two years.

As they spoke further, she confirmed that the clothes the man was wearing had been her husband's burial clothes. On verifying further, the signature matched that of her husband's as well. The only striking oddity that stood out was the difference in the voice of the man. Savalas later discovered that the man's high-pitched voice could be described as a result of his destroyed larynx, for he had committed suicide by shooting himself in the throat.

The Tortured Spirit of Oiwa

Of the most popular ghost stories, is that of a woman named Oiwa, made popular by the theatrical telling of the legend.

It is said that Oiwa was married to Lemon, a mean Samurai. When her father came to know of Lemon's treachery, Lemon killed him. As time passed, Lemon fell in love with his neighbours' granddaughter, in spite of being married with a child. In order to marry his new lady love, he tried to kill Oiwa by poisoning her. As fate would have it, the poison did not kill Oiwa, but it left her disfigured. Soon, Oiwa who was crippled by her condition and heartbreak due to her husband's betrayal and passed away under mysterious conditions.

Free to marry his "true love" now, Lemon arranged for Oiwa's death to look like she was having an affair with one of the servants, whom he killed and placed on a wooden door alongside his wife before throwing them into the river.

But oh, was he mistaken! Under the false belief that he was rid of Oiwa and was now free, Lemon married his lover. However, in a freaky turn of events, he now saw the disfigured face of his deceased wife on his new wife.

He picked up his sword and severed her neck, only to discover that he had killed his new wife instead. He killed his new father-in-law in the same fashion, mistaking him for the ghost of the servant he had so ruthlessly butchered.

Oiwa found her revenge at last, when her brother found Lemon in the mountains where he had fled to hide, and killed Lemon in his cabin.

Jason Keeler

The Ghost of Okiku

Yet another tale of vengeance, the tale of Okiku tells the story of how she found her revenge on her samurai master at last.

Okiku served Aoyama, who fell in love with her, but she didn't reciprocate his love. In order to get Okiku to be his, he tried to frame her for breaking plate number ten from his precious collection. He imposed a condition on her, according to which she would be forgiven and not shamed for her folly, if she agreed to love him.

When Okiku refused, Aoyama killed her with his bare hands. After he had killed her, Aoyama threw Okiku's corpse into the old well behind his home. After this incident, Aoyama could not sleep at nights as he was awoken with the sounds of Okiku's spirit breaking out into loud wails and sobbing after counting nine unbroken plates. Gradually, Aoyama lost his mind, and Okiku is said to have finally gotten her revenge.

Screaming Jenny of Harper's Ferry

Set during the time when people started to occupy the shacks abandoned by the B&O Railroad during the depression, this is a tale of a woman named Jenny who haunts the ferry to this day.

The people residing in such shacks would often build themselves fire pits for warmth during the winter. One such woman was named Jenny, and as she warmed herself near the fire one day, her dress caught fire. To put out the fire, she started to run, screaming, towards the railroad tracks and as a result, agitated the flames further. As she was running down the rail tracks, an approaching train saw her and tried to stop, but Jenny was run over.

Jenny was buried and the incident was laid to rest, when one day, an engineer saw a ball of fire down the tracks. The oncoming train then stopped in its tracks, but unlike with Jenny, there was nobody under the train.

Jenny's ghost is often sighted near Harper's ferry, engulfed in flames, resembling a ball of fire, usually accompanied with screaming.

Elisa Lam

In recent events, a frightening mystery has cropped up. It is the tale of Elisa Lam, a 21 year old student, who was found dead in a water supply tank in Los Angeles.

Elisa was found floating in one of the water tanks on the roof of the Cecil Hotel in L.A. Now imagine this- one day you complain of your water tasting weird, only to find out it has the body of a young woman dumped in it? Gross. But that is exactly how Elisa's body was discovered. Accidental drowning was ruled as the verdict, owing to lack of trauma on the victim's body.

How is this a horror story, you ask? Well, the eerie twist that this story takes is due to surveillance footage that was made public by the police. Not only was the roof barricaded completely with no access, the water tanks are reported to have been so heavy that they require to be cut open to be accessed. This leads to a failure in explaining how Lam could possibly have gotten in the tank and replaced the lid afterwards. No drugs or alcohol were found in Lam's system.

The Exorcism of Anneliese Michel

The popular movie "The Exorcism of Emily Rose" is loosely based on the accounts of Anneliese Michel, who began suffering from convulsions at the tender age of 16, leading to an extremely strong psychosis.

The convulsions first started in 1968, and by 1973, she had begun to hallucinate while praying. She reported visions of demonic faces in the day and claimed she heard voices that told her she was damned. The psychosis was severe, and led to unnatural behavior from her, such as ripping her clothes off, licking her own urine, eating coal and the like.

As time progressed, she became excessively averse to religious symbols, and could not consume holy water. As a result of her psychosis, she was transferred to a medical facility for psychiatric help. However, no amount of prescription drugs or treatment seemed to be of any help.

Tired of the failure of conventional medicine in treating Anneliese, her family decided to take matters into their own hands, and approached the Catholic Church instead. According to the church, she was suffering from demonic possession.

The clincher? Her condition did not improve, even after seventy six exorcisms; rather she reacted very violently to them. Her life eventually gave out due to starvation, as she refused to eat.

The Famous Ghost of Mercy Lena Brown

This is a tale of the crazily superstitious- and how. In the 1700s and early 1800s, Rhode Island villagers began to believe that the reason for the untimely death and sudden demise of their loved ones was because the sick were being targeted by evil forces.

They also developed the belief that the ones who had died would return to the living at night to suck the vitality out of them. Owing to this belief, the villagers starting practicing the routine of exhuming graves, burning the heart and drinking the ashes mixed with water to free themselves from the curse of the evil spirits.

After Mercy Lena Brown's death, her own father followed this ritual. It has been said, that ever since the villagers first desecrated her grave, her ghost has been seen and heard in places, by many people. Her corpse, without the heart, is buried in Chestnut Hill Cemetery in Exeter, Rhode Island.

Those who have visited have reported sightings of her ghost, odd blue lights in the cemetery, and the distinct scent of roses after they have prayed for Mercy. Instead of being a vengeful and formidable spirit, Mercy Lena Brown is said to be a compassionate local ghost.

The Legend of Octavia Hatcher

This is one of the saddest spooky stories I have come across, and you'll soon know why. In January 1981, Octavia Hatcher contracted a mysterious affliction after giving birth to her firstborn, Jacob. Soon after being born, Jacob passed away and that led Octavia to depression. Doctors could not cure her as she advanced to a much

worse, comatose state. She died on May 2' or so the locals believed.

Eerily enough, within a few days of her demise, some locals started to experience a similar affliction and drifted into a coma-like state. It was later confirmed that this state was due to the bite of the tsetse fly. These bites lead to a comatose condition in the patient, though they just sort of passed off in that state but would wake up eventually.

Octavia's husband realized that Octavia may have contracted the same sickness and may not have been dead, just in a comatose. He ordered for an exhumation and what they found when they dug out her casket was truly heart breaking yet spooky. Octavia was indeed buried alive and after being buried, she woke up from the comatose state and realized she was buried. They saw her body marked with scratches, placing asphyxiation as her cause of death, while she had clearly tried to escape from the grave.

Gut wrenching, eerie and spooky! That is all I can say about this incident.

Major Graham Mansion

The foundation for Major Graham Mansion was a log cabin in Wytheville, built by Joseph Baker in the late 1700s. The ghosts that are said to haunt the Major Graham mansion are said to be those of Joseph Baker and two of his slaves.

To end their slavery soon, and be released, the two slaves decided to end Joseph Baker's life, for he promised the slaves freedom on his demise. They murdered their owner and added him to a corn mash. However, their plans of going scot free were thwarted, as the news of their crime spread and they were captured. The slaves were hanged to death on the property itself. Now, the locals strongly believe in sightings and apparitions of three ghosts that haunt the site.

The property was eventually purchased by Major Graham, who employed many slaves for the construction of the Mansion. People believe that he was greatly oppressive towards his slaves, and had cages, chains and even guillotines in his mansion to punish those who defied him. Many slaves were killed on this property and even their ghosts are known to wander the property.

Among the paranormal presences on this property, there are sightings of the ghosts of several others enslaved during the times of Major Graham, which have been caught on video and EVPs.

Conclusion

With this, we now come to the end of this spook fest. Now, I don't know if you are a horror buff or someone mildly interested in things of a spooky nature, but I do hope that you enjoyed the book thoroughly.

Delving into the unknown, the unexplained, and the strange is thrilling, and a lot of fun. And what better than reading about true horror stories to do so? Well, whether or not you believe in them, now you know a few good stories to tell your friends and family- or the people you don't like so much, whom you want to frighten.

In the book, I have spoken about haunted buildings, frightening forests and creepy incidents to make any horror lovers day, I hope you liked the stories and got the same chill I got when I wrote them.

I hope you enjoyed this book, thank you and good luck!

Check Out My Other Books

Below you'll find some of my other popular books that are popular on Amazon and Kindle as well. You can visit my author page on Amazon to see other work done by me. (Jason Keeler).

Murder Mysteries

Missing Persons

True Ghost Stories

True Ghost Stories – Volume 2

Cannibal Killers

Cannibal Killers – Volume 2

True Murder Stories

Unexplained Disappearances

Unexplained Disappearances – Volume 2

Serial Killers

You can simply search for these titles on the Amazon website with my name to find them.

LIBRARY BUGS BOOKS

CPSIA information can be obtained
at www.ICGtesting.com
Printed in the USA
LVHW101002160522
718889LV00004B/140

9 781530 070732